OUTDOOR
ADVENTURE PACK

SURVIVAL TIPS AND TRICKS FOR BEGINNERS

MARC SUMERAK

CONTENTS

INTRODUCTION

SURVIVAL ISN'T EASY.

No matter who you are or where you may be, each and every day is full of unique challenges that must be conquered if you hope to endure and thrive. In some extreme situations, however, the essential skills required to survive don't come quite so naturally.

That's where this book comes in, to help teach you exactly what you need to know to make it through even the most unexpected and unforgiving circumstances. In these pages, you'll learn how to make a shelter, build a fire, locate clean water, forage for food, protect yourself from bad weather, and find your way back home safely afterwards.

Whether you're lost in the wilderness or buried by an avalanche, knowing these essential emergency survival skills could literally mean the difference between life and death. They may not make the situation you're in any less frightening, but they will give you a better chance of living to tell the tale.

ABOUT THIS KIT

This kit includes items that will be a huge help on any outdoor adventure.

COMPASS WITH CARABINER:

Essential for navigation, a compass will help you orient yourself in the wilderness.

10-IN-1 MULTI-TOOL:

Small enough to store in your wallet, this mighty multi-tool has many uses.

PARACORD BRACELET:

This lightweight bracelet unwinds into a sturdy 9 foot (2.75M) long paracord. You can use it for helpful knotwork (p. 10) and shelter building (p. 14).

FLINT-STRIKER:

Use this essential tool to start a fire. Strike the two pieces together to generate sparks that can ignite kindling.

GUIDANCE STICKERS:

These bright, arrow-shaped stickers are useful to mark natural landmarks to let yourself and others know which direction you are heading.

REFLECTIVE SHEET:

Use this sheet in the book to signal an SOS.

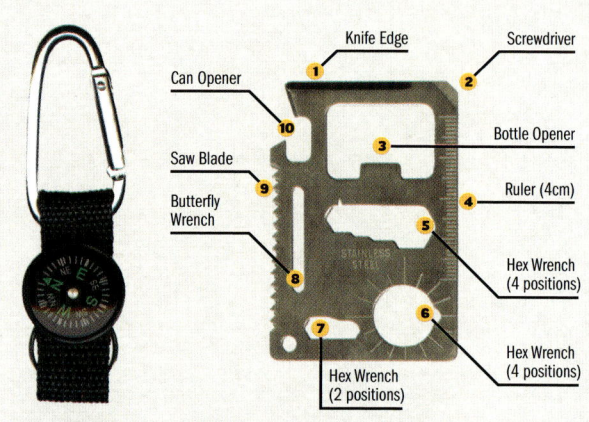

Knife Edge — 1
Can Opener — 10
Saw Blade — 9
Butterfly Wrench — 8
Hex Wrench (2 positions) — 7
Screwdriver — 2
Bottle Opener — 3
Ruler (4cm) — 4
Hex Wrench (4 positions) — 5
Hex Wrench (4 positions) — 6
STAINLESS STEEL

OTHER ITEMS TO PACK IN YOUR BACKPACK

TENT:
The simplest shelter solution, tents come in many easy-to-carry varieties.

SLEEPING BAG:
A nice, cozy bedroll is a must for keeping warm on long, cold nights in the wild.

TARP:
A plastic tarp can be used to cover the ground in your tent or to create a makeshift shelter. A clear tarp can even be used to build a solar still. (See Page 26.)

WATER:
Start your trip with a few full water bottles, and be sure to have filters to purify emergency water sources. (See Page 22.)

FOOD:
Bring enough food and snacks for your trip, plus a little extra, just in case. But be sure to properly store it so that you don't attract animals. (See Page 20.)

FIRST AID KIT:
You never plan to get hurt, but be ready if you do with the proper bandages and medications. (See Page 40.)

SURVIVAL

FLASHLIGHT:

A good fire will provide a lot of light at your campsite, but a strong flashlight is a must-have for navigating dark, unfamiliar terrain when you need to venture further afield. A headlamp leaves your hands free to cook, make a fire, or navigate your surroundings more easily.

SWISS ARMY KNIFE:

This popular multi-tool has tons of essential items packed into its tiny body, with most larger versions including a can opener, bottle opener, corkscrew, screwdrivers, file, and, of course, a selection of blades.

HATCHET:

A small handheld hatchet can be invaluable if you need to split firewood, chop down branches to build a shelter, or cut any other items that might be too thick for your knife.

SHOVEL:

Sure, you can dig with your hands, but a small hand shovel makes the job so much easier. Shovels can help you extinguish a fire, dig an emergency shelter, or even reach an underground water source.

TOOLS

BINOCULARS:
If you're not sure what awaits you off in the distance, binoculars can give you a better look without having to get up close and personal.

RADIO:
The wilderness may seem isolated, but a battery-powered radio can offer a small taste of the world back home. If you can get a signal, you'll have access to weather reports and some great tunes!

TWO-WAY RADIOS:
A different type of radio altogether, the two-way radio—or walkie-talkie—is a great option when you're braving the wild with a friend, allowing you to keep in contact if you get separated.

KNOW YOUR KNOTS

There are hundreds of different ways to tie a knot, but the ones pictured here are some of the most useful and effective in a survival situation.

SQUARE KNOT:

This *joining* knot is a simple way to tie two ends of a rope together or to link two separate pieces of equally thick rope. It's useful for tying up a bundle, and is often used in first aid. It's called a square knot because it looks like it has four sides to it.

Step One:
Place the left strand over the right strand.

Step Two:
Pull the left strand around the back and through the loop you created.

Step Three:
Now cross the right strand over the left strand.

Step Four:
Pull the right strand around the back and through the new loop you just created, and tighten.

BOWLINE:

The bowline (BO-lin) creates a loop at the end of a rope that won't change size or slip. You can tie it around yourself—or another person—in a rescue situation.

Step One:
Create a loop in the left side of the rope (top over bottom).

Step Two:
Feed the right strand up through the loop.

Step Three:
Bring the right strand around the back of the left strand and feed it down into the loop. Tighten!

CLOVE HITCH:

The clove hitch is a quick, easy knot that can secure your line to a post, tree, or carabiner.

Step One:
Wrap the rope around an object, then bring the rope around a second time above the first wrap.

Step Two:
As you bring the rope around to the front, feed it through the loop you just created.

Step Three:
Tighten by pulling hard on the two strands, being sure to push the two loops together.

CHOOSING A CAMPSITE

Before you can consider pitching a tent or building a shelter, you'll need to locate a good site. There are a lot of factors to consider when searching for the perfect campsite, so be sure to take the following into account:

TEMPERATURE:

The higher the temperature outside, the more likely you'll want to set up camp at a lower altitude. But to get a little extra warmth when the temperature is low, set up camp on a sunny hillside or near a large exposed rock that will absorb heat.

WATER ACCESS:

Campsites should have easy access to water, but setting up right on the side of a riverbank or lake could make you more vulnerable to bites from the bugs that breed there, attacks by the animals that drink there, and rising water levels. Make sure water is nearby, but always keep a safe distance.

MOISTURE LEVEL:

No one wants a damp camp, as wetness rapidly reduces body heat. Make your camp on dry, level ground, avoiding areas that have poor drainage or could collect standing water.

VISIBILITY:

Making your camp near a trail or on the side of a hill will allow more visibility of your surroundings and might also allow anyone searching for you to locate you more easily.

POTENTIAL HAZARDS:

There are enough dangers out there already, so don't make it worse by choosing shelter in a high-risk area. Avoid steep slopes and any areas that might flood or threaten rock slides.

TRAIL TIP

Allow yourself plenty of time to find and set up your campsite. If you wait until it gets dark or you get tired, you'll have to settle for a less-than-ideal location.

PITCHING A TARP

You don't need an elaborate store-bought tent that instantly assembles itself. With a tarp, some rope, and a few well-placed sticks, you can create your own tent in no time at all. Just follow these simple steps:

STEP ONE:

Tie a line of rope or wire between two trees. If you can't find two trees close enough together near your campsite of choice, find two sturdy branches and drive them into the ground to use as upright poles.

STEP TWO:

Drape the tarp over the line, so that the tarp is folded in half.

STEP THREE:

Tie shorter lines to each of the four corners of the tarp.

STEP FOUR:

Create stakes using small branches and tie them to the corner lines. Drive the stakes into the ground, stretching the tarp out to create an "A-Frame" shape.

ALTERNATE OPTION:

Instead of stakes, you can also weigh down the corners of your tarp with heavy rocks or logs.

TENT TIPS

→ You can maximize your coverage and protection by suspending your shelter's center line closer to the ground.

→ There are dozens of other variations of tarp tents, including pyramids and tepees, so be creative and build the one that's best for you.

→ Tarps can also add an extra layer of waterproofing or groundcover to a store-bought tent.

COMMON CAMPFIRES

TEEPEE FIRE:

A teepee fire is the easiest and most common type of campfire to build. First, take any tinder twigs and bend them in half, creating an up-side-down V shape. Put it on the ground and place any other tinder material—dried grass, leaves, paper, etc.—beneath it. Light the tinder with a match. As the tinder begins to burn, start to place a few twigs around it in that familiar tepee shape, leaning against each other at the top for support. Start with just a few pieces of kindling and add more as the fire starts to catch, filling in the gaps as you go. Finally, using the same process, start adding the fuel wood to create an even larger tepee.

LOG CABIN:

Building a log cabin fire isn't that different from building an actual log cabin. Start with two pieces of kindling running parallel, about six inches (15 cm) apart. Next, stack two more parallel pieces on top running in the opposite direction, creating a square shape. Alternate a few layers back and forth until you have a solid structure. Add some tinder to the center, light it, then cover the top of the structure with small tinder twigs.

PLATFORM:

A wonderful fire for cooking and creating hot coals, the platform fire is similar in structure to the log cabin fire, but each alternating layer should have multiple pieces of wood placed side-by-side, creating a solid surface. The largest logs should be placed on the bottom, and the wood should gradually get smaller as you go up. Tinder is then lit on top of the structure and the fire burns down to the bottom.

STAR:

The star fire is a low-maintenance, long-burning fire great for situations where good fuel wood may not be abundant. Start a small tepee fire and surround it with three to five large logs arranged in a circular pattern with their ends pointing outward. As the logs burn down, push them in closer to the fire to keep it burning strong.

LEAN-TO:

Great for windy or rainy situations, the lean-to fire uses a natural barrier to protect your fire's early stages from the elements. Place your tinder on the ground directly beside a rock or a large green log, then place a layer of kindling over it at an angle, with one end on the ground and the other propped up by the barrier. Add a few more layers of kindling in the same slanted manner, followed by layers of fuel.

LIGHTING A FIRE

You may have built the best-looking pile of logs in history, but unless you know a way to get a fire started, it won't do you any good. Here are a few great options to get things burning:

MATCHES:

Perhaps the simplest method of fire starting, matches provide a flame with a single strike. Invest in waterproof matches if you can. They'll be a huge help if you and your pack unexpectedly get caught in the rain.

FLINT AND STEEL:

This method is an old standard, where a piece of tempered high-carbon steel is struck against a piece of flint to generate an intensely hot spark. The spark only lasts for a fraction of a second, so be sure to keep it close to your tinder. Once the spark causes the tinder to smolder, blow on it until you get a flame.

STEEL WOOL AND BATTERIES:

Steel wool is good for more than just scrubbing your pans at the end of a camping trip. Stretch out a six-inch (15 cm) length of super-fine wool and touch it with both the positive and negative leads on a battery. This should create a short but intense sparking glow across the wool. Avoid holding the wool itself, as it will get extremely hot!

FRICTION FIRE:

Friction creates heat, and heat can lead to fire. Sadly, lighting a fire isn't as simple as rubbing two sticks together, but you can create a fire plow by carving a rut into a two-foot-long (about 60 cm) piece of soft wood and quickly and repeatedly scraping a hardwood stick down that path. The resulting pile of wood dust should eventually combust—if your arms don't tire out first.

THE SUN:

The sun is a giant ball of fire in the sky, so why not use it to create a significantly smaller fire in your camp? Focus the power of the sun via convex lenses (like the ones in eyeglasses, binoculars, magnifying glasses, or cameras), aiming the resulting concentrated hotspot at your tinder. You can even polish the bottom of a soda can with a chocolate bar for an ultra-reflective surface that will create the same effect!

CRITTER-FREE CAMPSITES

No matter where you camp, you'll probably run into some form of wildlife. They may be interested in you, but they're likely far more interested in all the delicious-smelling things you brought with you. Even the tiniest creatures can create havoc in camp, so take the following precautions.

→ Never feed the animals. If they know you've got delicious things, they'll assume you have more to share. Curious critters have no qualms about turning your camp upside down to find what they are looking for.

→ Store any food in a properly sealed container. There are even camping storage bins available that are designed specifically to eliminate food odors and prevent animals with crafty paws from opening them.

→ Hide surplus food safely out of sight. Once some animals identify a food container, they'll look for other similar containers and smash them open to get what they want.

→ Suspend your food from a tree. If it's in a sealed container, the animals probably won't notice it's there—but just to be safe, don't suspend it directly above your camp!

→ Don't use any scented lotions, soaps, or deodorants. To animals, all good smells are attractive, whether they come from food or not.

→ Keep a clean camp. Your garbage and food scraps are just as tantalizing to wild animals as your freshly cooked dinner. Seal all garbage in an odor-proof bag for proper disposal later.

→ For even better protection, cook your meals and clean your gear a safe distance (about 200 feet—60 m) from your camp.

FINDING WATER

Clean drinking water is something we tend to take for granted. At home, a cool, refreshing drink comes as easily as turning on a faucet or opening a bottle. But in the wild, it might take a bit more work to find a suitable source of hydration.

➜ When your mouth starts getting parched, trust your ears to help you find a nearby water source. Stand still to eliminate any noise you might be generating and listen for the sound of rushing water.

➜ If there are no rivers, waterfalls, or streams around, follow these other signs to lead you in the right direction:

  ➜ Groups of animal tracks that converge on well-worn paths may lead to watering holes.

  ➜ Birds often circle over bodies of water.

  ➜ An increase in the number of insects can be a sign of water nearby, as many species breed near wet areas.

➜ If the local fauna aren't cluing you in, head downhill. Thanks to gravity, water naturally flows down into valleys and channels. The lower you get, the more likely you will be to find water.

➜ If you can't find even a puddle, look for damp soil. It's worth digging to see if you can find an underground water source. Groundwater tends to be heavily polluted, but in a survival scenario, muddy water is better than no water.

➜ Even if your water source seems clear and pristine, you should properly treat the water before drinking it.

PURIFICATION

Finding water is just the first step. Even if you've located a water source, there's no guarantee that the water itself is actually safe to drink. Untreated water can carry all sorts of deadly microbes and parasites that can actually *increase* your rate of dehydration if they make it into your system. To avoid consuming contaminated water, always purify your water using one of the following methods before drinking it.

FILTERS:

Portable water filters designed specifically for wilderness situations are widely available. These specialized pumps are capable of removing dirt and most harmful bacteria. Still, some waterborne viruses may be small enough to sneak through even the tiniest pores, so additional chemical treatment may be required if the water source is suspect.

TRAIL TIP

Some water bottles come with a powerful filter built into their lids, allowing you to scoop up water on the go and drink it without any special processing or treatment.

TABLETS AND DROPS:

There are a number of commercially available purification tablets on the market, as well as chemical drops used to kill any diseases present in the water. These treatments use small doses of chemicals like chlorine or iodine, which can be dangerous to consume in large quantities, so be sure to read the instructions very carefully for the proper amounts to use. Chemical treatments often take a while to work before you can drink the water, and they can also make the water taste bad.

BOILING:

The most foolproof way to make sure that your water is free of any harmful biological contaminants is to boil it. Place water in a pot over your campfire and let it reach a rolling boil. Since recommended boiling times can vary depending on your altitude, it's best to play it safe and boil the water for a full ten minutes. It won't clean any dirt out of your water, nor will it be terribly refreshing until it cools down substantially, but it will certainly kill any bacteria or viruses lurking in the liquid.

ALTERNATIVE WATER SOURCES

Streams and ponds are great water sources when you can find them, but there are plenty of other ways to find water in nature. As with all water sources, it is always recommended that any water collected in nature be properly purified (using the methods discussed on Pages 22-23) before drinking.

RAINWATER:

Occasionally, bad weather can bring very good things. One of the fastest ways to gather water in the wild is to collect rainwater. Set out as many clean containers as you can during a storm to gather a large supply. You can even make temporary containers by stretching sheets of plastic into bowl-like shapes.

DEW:

The condensation that settles on leaves, blades of grass, and tree limbs in the early morning hours can be another great source of water. Tie some absorbent cloth (like a T-shirt, towel, or bandana) around your legs, walk through areas of tall grass, and then wring the collected dew into a container.

Despite what old cowboy movies suggest, the liquid found inside most desert cacti is not safe to drink, and can actually be quite poisonous.

TRANSPIRATION:

Transpiration is the process in which plants naturally release water vapor into the air during photosynthesis. If you tie a plastic bag around a plant or a leafy limb of a tree, the vapor it releases will become trapped inside the bag and condense on its walls. The condensation will then run down to the lowest point in the bag, creating a small pool of water.

SNOW:

If you're in a snowy region, you're in luck, because the ground is already covered in frozen water. But be careful: snow and ice can be great sources of hydration—but only if you melt them first! Consuming them in their frozen state drastically lowers the body's temperature and can actually lead to dehydration and hypothermia.

SOLAR STILL

When fresh water is seemingly nowhere to be found, building a still might be the only answer to ensure adequate hydration. This simple two-part system uses the sun to draw the moisture out of your natural surroundings, distilling it into pure, drinkable water.

A makeshift solar still can be created using only two items—a clear plastic sheet and a small, clean container—plus a few rocks. Here's how to build it:

STEP ONE:

Dig a pit in an area that gets a lot of direct sunlight. The size of the pit is determined by the size of your plastic sheet. You should be able to completely cover the pit with the sheet. The larger your pit, the quicker you'll be able to collect a large volume of water.

STEP TWO:

Place the small container in the middle of the pit. This could be a bucket, a drinking glass, or anything that will be able to hold water.

STEP THREE:

Cover the pit with the plastic sheet. A great option is a plastic drop cloth used for groundcover in a tent, but you could even use a clear plastic rain poncho.

STEP FOUR:
Anchor the plastic sheet in place by putting rocks around the outer edges.

STEP FIVE:
Place a small rock in the center of the sheet, directly above the container, to weigh it down and create an inverted cone shape.

STEP SIX:
Let the sun do the rest. The heat passing through the plastic will evaporate any moisture below it, transforming it into vapor. That vapor rises, but gets trapped beneath the plastic. The vapor then condenses on the plastic, turning back into water droplets, which run down the slope of the weighted sheet and drip into the container below.

SMART DISTILLING

→ Distilling water removes the majority of dirt, metals, pathogens, and pollutants, creating a very safe source of drinking water.

→ Under the right conditions, a good still can generate up to a quart of water in a 24-hour period.

→ You can use this same process to draw fresh water out of salt water. Instead of digging a pit, place the sheet above a large bowl of salt water with your empty container in the center.

EDIBLE PLANTS

If you're stranded in the wilderness and you've eaten your last can of beans and your entire supply of protein bars, don't worry. While your favorites vegetables may not grow freely in the wild, it's likely that there are plenty of delicious alternatives sprouting up all around you.

BERRIES:

The forest is full of wild berries, but many of them can be extremely poisonous. It's best to stick with ones that you can easily identify, such as blackberries, raspberries, and strawberries. As a rule of thumb, steer clear of white and yellow berries, as only about 10 percent of those are edible. The darker the berry, the more likely it can be safely consumed.

DANDELIONS:

It's easy to recognize the bright yellow flowers of the dandelion—especially if you constantly battle to keep them off a perfectly mowed lawn. But these pesky weeds are completely edible from stem to flower and are packed full of vitamins. Their naturally bitter taste can be reduced if you boil them.

CLOVER:

You don't need to find a four-leafed version of this common plant to be lucky. A member of the pea family, clover can be eaten raw or cooked. It's another good source of vitamins, and the flowers make a nice tea. It's clear why honeybees love this common ground cover.

CATTAILS:

Typically found near the edges of swampy areas, the cattail is a versatile plant that has long been dubbed the "supermarket of the wild." Most of the plant is edible, but the lower white area of the stalk and the plant's roots tend to be favorites. Even the corn-dog-shaped flowers can be eaten, though you might want to save them and dry them out, as they make great tinder for your fire.

TRAIL TIP

Just because a bird or animal can safely eat something doesn't mean a human can. Always err on the side of caution!

POISONOUS
PLANTS

While nature's bounty is abundant, there are plenty of plants whose natural defenses make them extremely dangerous to anyone who consumes them. They may look delicious, but these poisonous plants might prove to be the last meal you ever order.

HEMLOCK:

A member of the wild carrot family, hemlock looks quite similar to its edible cousins. However, the toxins that reside in the plant's roots have earned it the designation of "the deadliest plant in North America." Two common varieties of hemlock, poison hemlock and water hemlock, can cause seizures and death when ingested—or even touched!

DEADLY NIGHTSHADE:

Although darker berries generally tend to be the safest, there's one pitch-black berry that may actually be the most toxic of all—the deadly nightshade. Ingesting even a few berries of the deadly nightshade, also known as belladonna, will lead to delirium, disorientation, and death. The berries aren't the only culprits, as the plant's leaves are poisonous as well.

RHUBARB:

Its celery-like stalks may make a great addition to desserts, but the leaves of the rhubarb plant are highly toxic. Consuming these leafy greens—whether raw or cooked—can lead to weakness, difficulty breathing, burning sensations, internal bleeding, and even death. Think about that the next time you order a slice of strawberry-rhubarb pie!

MUSHROOMS:

Much like berries, there are just as many poisonous mushrooms as there are safe ones. Unlike berries, however, the edible varieties are a lot more difficult to identify for an amateur forager. In general, it's probably best to steer clear of any fungus.

NATURE'S MEDICINE

Plants can be used as far more than just a good source of nutrition. Many wild plants and herbs can also help to cure common ailments. If you have developed any health concerns during your time in the wild, look around you for these natural remedies.

LAVENDER:

This familiar-smelling plant has been used throughout history to soothe all sorts of skin problems, including bug bites, rashes, and burns. Just crush the leaves and apply them to the affected area. Lavender also makes for a great natural bug repellent!

CATNIP:

It might not make you run around in a frenzy like it does for cats, but catnip does have a surprising effect on humans. A tea made from the leaves of the catnip plant has the ability to induce sweating, which is one way to reduce a fever.

YARROW:

Although its flowers look more like a big cluster of mini daisies, yarrow is part of the sunflower family. There's seemingly nothing yarrow can't do, but at the top of the list is wound healer: it can stop the bleeding of minor cuts and abrasions, and has the added benefit of being a pain reliever with antibacterial properties.

BUTTERFLY WEED:

Did you eat something that you're suddenly starting to regret? Follow it with a bit of butterfly weed to get it out of your system. The milky sap from the plant is an emetic, which means it stimulates vomiting. Throwing up isn't fun, but it's better than having a belly full of poisonous berries!

TRAIL TIP

A tea made from the leaves of blackberry plants can be used to ease stomach discomfort, including diarrhea.

SNAKEBITES!

If you're bitten by any snake in the wild, it won't be pleasant. But if you're bitten by a venomous species, it could very well prove fatal if not treated properly and quickly. If you're exploring a region that is the natural habitat of venomous snakes, it's important to know how to keep clear of potential danger—and what to do if you can't.

AVOIDING SNAKEBITES:

Since you're probably not carrying a supply of antivenom with you, your best bet is to learn how to avoid bites at all costs. Here's how:

→ Stay on trails and avoid tall grass and underbrush.

→ Wear tall boots and long pants when hiking to create a strong bite barrier.

→ Don't ever touch a snake, even if it looks dead.

→ Inspect logs and rocks before picking them up, and look into holes or cracks before reaching into them.

→ Zip up your tent at night and check your boots before putting them on.

TREATING SNAKEBITES:

If you get a venomous snakebite, seek immediate medical attention, if possible. Before that:

→ Wash the wound with soap and water as soon as possible.

→ Keep the wound below heart level.

→ Take off any jewelry near the bite in case of swelling.

→ Wrap a tight bandage above the bite to slow circulation and the spread of venom.

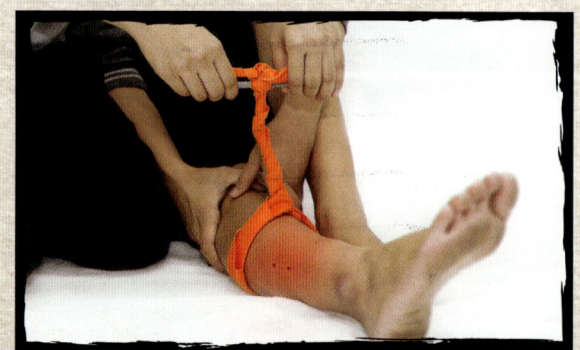

REMOVING A
TICK

DEER TICKS:

Commonly found in wooded areas during warmer seasons, ticks are notorious for carrying a large number of disease-causing bacteria, viruses, and parasites. From Lyme disease to Rocky Mountain spotted fever, a tick bite on you or an animal companion can have long-lasting effects if not quickly and properly treated.

REMOVING A TICK:

→ Grasp the tick as close to the surface of your skin as possible, using tweezers. Avoid squeezing the tick, as it could release infected fluid into your body.

→ Pull the tick up and away in one steady motion. If you jerk or twist, the tick's head might pull off and remain embedded in your skin.

→ Once the tick is fully removed, clean the bite with rubbing alcohol or soap and water.

→ Keep the tick in a sealed jar full of rubbing alcohol or in an airtight bag, just in case it needs to be examined later.

→ If you develop a rash, pain, or any flu-like symptoms, seek medical attention.

TRAIL TIP

Ticks tend to reside in wooded areas with tall grasses and shrubs. If you keep on a clear part of the trail and avoid brushing up against foliage, you're less likely to have one of these awful arachnids hitch a ride home on your skin

BLIZZARDS

If you're caught in a blizzard—an intense snowstorm with winds above 35 miles per hour (56 kph) and less than a quarter mile of visibility—you may find yourself stuck in one place due to a rapidly accumulating pile of precipitation. Here are some hot tips for braving a winter whiteout.

→ First, look for shelter. If there isn't a man-made building nearby, you may have to build a makeshift shelter yourself.

→ Build a small fire to keep yourself warm and to fight off hypothermia and frostbite. Make sure to surround the fire with rocks to radiate extra heat.

→ Stay hydrated by melting any snow before drinking it (to avoid hypothermia and dehydration).

→ If you are stuck in a car, stay inside the parked vehicle—but be sure to clear an area behind the tailpipe so that exhaust fumes don't pollute your air

TRAIL TIP

If you're lucky enough to be indoors when a blizzard hits, stay there until the snow has passed. It's better to dig yourself out later than to find yourself without a way back in now.

AVALANCHES

Snow doesn't just fall—sometimes it slides. An avalanche occurs when large quantities of ice and snow rapidly descend down a steep slope, and it can be completely devastating to anything or anyone in its way. If you are unfortunate enough to be caught in an avalanche's path, you'll need to think fast.

→ If the ground starts to move, try to jump upslope first. If you accidentally caused the slide, you might have a chance to leap beyond its starting point to safety.

→ If the avalanche is coming from above you, move quickly toward the side of the slope. If you act fast, you may be able to get safely out of the way

→ Drop your equipment. Heavy gear will just slow you down.

→ Grab ahold of something sturdy. A tree or a big rock might anchor you in place until the danger passes.

→ If you get swept away by the rush of snow, try to swim with the current. Focus on keeping your head above the surface.

IF YOU START TO GET BURIED IN THE SNOW:

→ Keep one arm straight up towards the sky so you know which direction to dig to freedom.

→ Put the other hand over your mouth to capture air, then use it to dig an air pocket around your face.

FOLLOW THE STARS

If you can't find a specific star in the sky to follow, the motion of any star can tell you which way you're going. As the Earth naturally rotates throughout the night, stars slowly seem to make their way across the sky. Noticing where they're going can help you get headed back in the right direction.

STEP ONE:

Put two sticks into the ground, approximately three feet (not quite 1 m) apart.

STEP TWO:

Pick a bright star in the sky and sit in a place where that bright star looks as if it is aligned with the top of both sticks.

STEP THREE:

Watch the star for about thirty minutes. As the Earth rotates, it will seem as though the star has moved. The direction it seemingly moves determines the direction you're facing.

→ You're facing north if the star shifts to the left.

→ You're facing south if the star shifts to the right.

→ You're facing east if the star shifts up above the top of the sticks.

→ You're facing west if the star shifts down below the top of the sticks.

TRAIL TIP

Stay in one place. If you get up, the chances that you'll return to the exact same vantage point are slim, so you might not get an accurate read on the star's motion.

FIRST AID KIT

No one should head off on an adventure without a first aid kit in their pack. When braving the wild, it's almost a guarantee that someone is bound to get an injury—whether it's just a minor scrape, a bad splinter, or something far more serious. No matter what the ailment, having the right treatment on hand can prevent infection and ease the pain until you can get things properly checked out.

FIRST AID KIT ITEMS:

BANDAGES:

The wilderness is full of unexpected ways to get injured, so having adhesive bandages in various shapes and sizes is a great way to protect small wounds. Also, be sure to include gauze pads, a gauze roll, and medical tape to wrap larger cuts, and moleskin to cushion blisters.

OINTMENTS:

While a bandage might keep a wound clean, it won't necessarily prevent infection. Applying an antiseptic cream will fight off any bacteria and aid in healing. Also, bring burn ointment to help ease pain from prolonged sun exposure and minor fire-related mishaps.

Seal any medicines and ointments that are strong-smelling in a plastic bag within your first aid kit to avoid attracting animals. This will also protect from leakage.

MEDICATIONS:

Every first aid kit should include basic medications, including pain relievers (such as aspirin) and antihistamines. Personal medications should be packed as needed. These can include daily vitamins, prescription medications, and even EpiPens for those with severe allergies.

TOOLS:

Although most of your essential tools were already included in your pack, you may need a few extras for your first aid kit. Tweezers help to remove splinters and ticks. Scissors help to cut bandages (and string for your tent). A magnifying glass can help you find small debris in a wound. Even nail clippers and a needle and thread come in handy more often than you'd expect.

STERILIZATION:

If you're using tools for medical reasons, it's important to make sure that they are clean. Washing them with rubbing alcohol or hydrogen peroxide first will make sure that they are sterile and ready to use.

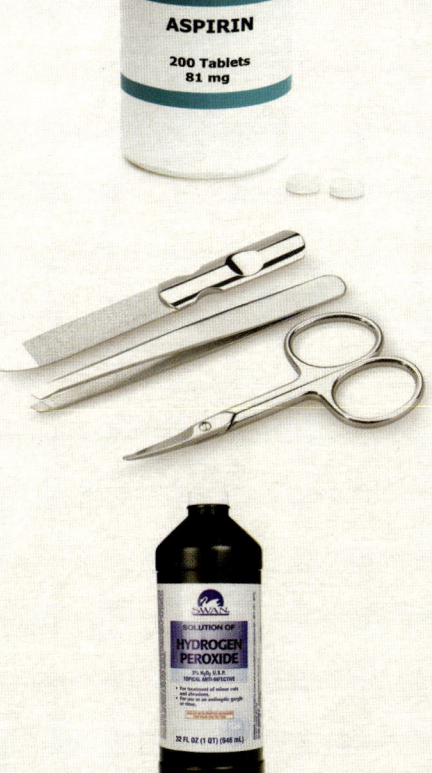

HEATSTROKE

Extreme temperatures can have powerful negative effects on the human body. It doesn't matter whether you're too hot or too cold; either way, the effects could be devastating if not caught early and treated properly.

Heatstroke, also known as hyperthermia, is a condition that occurs when the body's core temperature goes higher than 104 degrees Fahrenheit (40° C). It results from long periods of exposure to or increased physical activity in very hot environments. Symptoms of heatstroke include severe headache, physical weakness, light-headedness, shallow breathing, and hot, red, dry skin. These symptoms are accompanied by a noticeable lack of sweat, due to dehydration.

If you suspect that a companion might be suffering from heatstroke, it is important to call for medical assistance immediately. Once help is on the way, try the following to reduce the person's body temperature and prevent the condition from worsening:

→ Get them to a shady area and remove any heavy clothing they may be wearing.

→ Wet their skin with cool water from a damp towel or sponge.

→ Submerge their body in cool water, such as a lake, stream, or tub. Be sure to support their head above water in case they are too weak to do so themselves.

→ If ice is available, apply it to areas of the body with a high concentration of blood vessels (such as the neck, back, groin, and armpits).

HYPOTHERMIA

The opposite of hyperthermia is hypothermia, a condition where the body's core temperature drops below 82 degrees Fahrenheit (28° C). Hypothermia is caused by extended exposure to extremely low temperatures without proper protection. Symptoms include shallow breathing, weak pulse, disorientation, drowsiness, and intense shivering. Hypothermia can also cause confusion, which can prevent the victim from realizing the very real danger they are in. As with heatstroke, immediate medical attention is recommended for anyone suffering hypothermia. Before help arrives, attempt to gradually warm up their body using these methods:

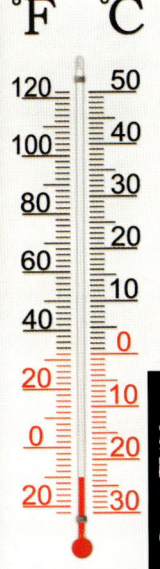

→ Get them indoors or to an area that is protected from the cold and remove any wet clothing they may be wearing.

→ Dry their skin and wrap them in blankets, towels, or dry clothing. Focus on warming their torso and head first.

→ Don't submerge them in warm water, as warming the body too quickly can cause other health problems.

→ If hot-water bottles or heating pads are available, wrap them in towels and apply them to the neck, chest, and groin.

BROKEN LIMBS

Accidents happen, even in the most controlled situations. In an unpredictable outdoor setting, the number of potential dangers that could lead to serious injury greatly increases. Nature trails don't come with safety rails, and misjudging one step on a steep path could lead to a fall that breaks more than just your confidence.

If you find yourself with a broken limb in the wild, here's what to do:

SET IT:

In most cases, you'll want to move a broken limb as little as possible to avoid doing any further damage. But in some more severe breaks, you might need to "set" the bone back in its proper position. Returning the bone to its natural alignment will help to reduce pain and prepare the limb for immobilization.

SPLINT IT:

Once the bone is oriented correctly, you'll need to prevent any further motion of the injured area. To achieve this, create a splint by using two sticks (as long as the limb and about one to two inches—2.5 to 5 cm—in diameter) placed on opposite sides of the limb. Secure the sticks in place with rope or pieces of cloth at the top and bottom of the limb, preventing it from moving or bending.

TREAT IT:

The best way to make sure a broken limb heals properly is to get to a hospital for immediate medical attention. While moving someone with a broken leg may require professional medical assistance, a person with a broken arm will likely be able to make it back to civilization safely on their own (though they may require a bit of extra help).

TRAIL TIP

Severe injuries can sometimes cause a person to go into a state of shock. If a companion with a broken limb suffers from an elevated heart rate, nausea, dizziness, chills, or starts to look pale, it's time to take a break and call for help. Keep them warm and hydrated (and off a broken leg) until assistance arrives.

PERFORMING CPR

If someone has stopped breathing, you may need to try to revive them using CPR, which stands for cardiopulmonary resuscitation. CPR is a basic skill that everyone should know, and there are courses available to become trained and certified in it. CPR could save a life in any number of everyday circumstances—from drownings to heart attacks.

STEP ONE:

Once you've determined that the victim is not breathing or responding, immediately call for medical assistance (if possible) before beginning to perform CPR.

STEP TWO:

Overlap your hands in the middle of the victim's chest and use your body weight to push down about two inches (5 cm). Repeat this at a rate of about two compressions (pushes) a second.

STEP THREE:

If you have CPR training, complete 30 compressions, and then gently tilt the victim's head back with one hand while lowering their chin with the other to open their airway. Check for any signs of breathing for five to ten seconds. NOTE: If you are not trained in CPR, continue with the "hands only" method described in Steps One and Two for 100 compressions before checking the victim's airway.

STEP FOUR:

If trained in CPR, move on to mouth-to-mouth breathing. Hold the victim's nose shut and make a seal around their mouth with your own. Blow a strong breath into their mouth for one second, followed by another. If their chest does not rise after the first breath, open their airway again (as described in Step Three) in case there is an obstruction.

STEP FIVE:

Following the two rescue breaths, begin the cycle over again—performing 30 chest compressions, checking the airway, and administering two rescue breaths—and repeat a total of five times. NOTE: If you are performing the "hands only" method, repeat five cycles of 100 chest compressions, checking the victim's airway between cycles.

STEP SIX:

If the victim is not breathing by the end of the fifth cycle, they may require other methods of resuscitation, such as a defibrillator. If you or someone else called for help, keep performing CPR until a professional arrives to offer assistance.

Brimming with creative inspiration, how-to projects, and useful information to enrich your everyday life, Quarto Knows is a favorite destination for those pursuing their interests and passions. Visit our site and dig deeper with our books into your area of interest: Quarto Creates, Quarto Cooks, Quarto Homes, Quarto Lives, Quarto Drives, Quarto Explores, Quarto Gifts, or Quarto Kids.

© 2021 Quarto Publishing Group USA Inc.

This edition published in 2021 by Chartwell Books, an imprint of The Quarto Group
142 West 36th Street, 4th Floor
New York, NY 10018 USA
T (212) 779-4972 F (212) 779-6058

www.Quarto.com

This book is part of the Outdoor Adventure Pack and is not to be sold separately.

21 22 23 24 25   5 4 3 2 1

ISBN: 978-0-7858-4051-0

Library of Congress Cataloging-in-Publication Data available upon request.

Author: Marc Sumerak

Printed, manufactured, and assembled in Shenzhen, China, 11/21.

Image credits:
All images and Graphic Elements © Shutterstock.com

Disclaimer text: You should NEVER put yourself in dangerous situations to test whether the advice in this book really works. The publisher cannot accept responsibility for any injuries, damage, loss, or prosecutions resulting from the information in this book.

355910